BE YOUR OWN BROKER (BYOB)

BECOMING A REAL ESTATE AGENT

V. SLATER

ISBN 9798865848004

For nearly two decades as a Real Estate Agent in the State of Michigan, I've navigated the complexities of the housing market, learning invaluable lessons along the way. In 2018, I channeled this knowledge and passion into founding Slater Signature Homes. Today, it's not just a brokerage—it's a testament to perseverance, evolving into a thriving six-figure business. Whether you're an emerging agent, an established professional, or intrigued by the intricacies of real estate, this account aims to inspire and inform.

Welcome aboard!

TABLE OF CONTENTS

AUTHOR BIO

In January 2006, I achieved a significant milestone which changed my life: passing the real estate exam. This marked the official initiation into the world of property dealings. It's not just about understanding property valuations or legal jargon; it's about the culmination of hard work, dedication, and a deep desire to succeed in this industry.

The subsequent step post-certification was diving headfirst into the field. By working for The Loft Warehouse in Downtown Detroit, a rich experience in dealing with condos, lofts, and other real estate opportunities in the downtown area was gained. This period was not just about executing transactions but about understanding the pulse of Detroit's property market, its evolution, and its people.

Being a successful Realtor isn't just about showcasing homes or closing deals; it's about understanding the heartbeat of a community. When I sift through newspaper articles every morning, it's not just headlines I see, but stories of families, developments, dreams, and concerns that will shape the future of neighborhoods. Delving into these stories helps me connect with the aspirations and fears of my clients. By observing neighborhood trends, I'm not merely tracking market dynamics but listening to the whispered tales of tree- lined streets, the laughter echoing from community parks, or the concerns of local schools. This personal touch, the ability to connect deeply with the communities I serve, is what has made my journey as a Realtor not just successful, but incredibly fulfilling.

By 2018, armed with a wealth of experience and a clear vision, it was time for an entrepreneurial leap. Slater Signature Homes Brokerage was born, symbolizing not just a business but the manifestation of years of learning and passion. This new venture was about more than just selling homes; it was about creating lasting relationships and leaving indelible marks on Detroit's real estate landscape.

The journey through the real estate industry is paved with challenges, learning, and boundless opportunities. From passing the real estate exam to establishing a successful brokerage, the path is a testament to dedication, perseverance, and a love for the craft. As this Ebook illustrates, with the right mindset and determination, anyone can carve out their own unique success story in the ever-evolving world of real estate.

INTRODUCTION

✓ *Have you always dreamt of becoming a real estate agent?*
✓ *Is it your dream to help people find their dream real estate properties, homes, or office spaces?*
✓ *Do you want to learn the necessary skills and strategies that can help you succeed in this lucrative and rewarding career?*

If so, reading this book will teach you everything you need to know to kick- start your journey as a real estate agent!

With average earnings of over $95,000 a year, which is over 60% of the national average across all occupations, there is no denying that being a real estate agent is rewarding.

Beyond its potentially high monetary rewards, you will meet successful people, experience the thrill of touring beautiful spaces, learn emerging trends in different real estate markets, know when there are good deals and opportunities in the real estate market, and so much more.

Alas, as the old saying goes, if wishes were horses, beggars would ride. Daydreaming about the glam of being a real estate agent is one thing; becoming a successful real estate agent who can earn commissions and have multiple potential deals lined up at a time is completely different.

Moreover, the industry is highly regulated, and you MUST have the necessary licenses and certifications.

The fact that you are here is evidence that you are considering becoming a real estate agent, have probably enrolled for the examination, or are considering enrolling for the certification course.

Perhaps you are looking for answers to the questions going through your mind. These questions may include the following:

- ✓ What does it take to pass the exam?
- ✓ What key topics should you excel in?
- ✓ What next after the exams – how do you get licensed?
- ✓ How do you become a seasoned real estate agent that has potential customers lined up?
- ✓ How do you decide what to specialize in?
- ✓ How do you become good at it?
- ✓ What then after succeeding?

You are about to discover answers to all these and related questions.

This book will walk you through the steps to getting started as a real estate agent, including choosing a niche, getting licensed, finding clients, marketing yourself, and growing your business.

More precisely, you will learn the following:

- How to ace the real estate exam and become a licensed agent
- The various requirements for real estate agents, such as education, experience, and fees for each state
- How to develop and master the most essential skills as a real estate agent
- Hacks and tips to becoming a seasoned agent, such as taking practice tests, reviewing key concepts, and managing your time and stress

- How to pick out the perfect real estate brokerage to work with
- And much more

Whether you are new to real estate or have experience in the field, this guide will help you take your career to the next level and achieve your professional goals.

Let's begin!

CHAPTER 1

REQUIREMENTS OF THE AGENT PRE-LICENSING COURSE

The pre-agent course is a mandatory education program you must complete before taking the exam. Each state has its standards for the course, which can differ in terms of the number of hours, topics covered, fees, and exam structure. Therefore, before you start, you must inform yourself of the criteria used.

You may be wondering: *What are my state's requirements for the pre- licensing agent course?*

The answer is not simple since each state has unique requirements for getting an`d keeping a real estate license. However, most states have a few things in common, such as the following:

- You must complete a certain number of hours of pre-licensing education from an approved provider. The number of hours varies from 40 to over 200, depending on the state.
- You must pass a state exam that covers real estate laws, principles, and practices.
- The state licensing body requires an application, which you must submit with a fee. Some states additionally perform background checks and require fingerprints.
- You must work under the supervision of a licensed broker when you start your career as a real estate agent. Also, you'll

need extra schooling, work experience, and exams to become a broker.

- You must complete continuing education courses every year or every few years. Continuing education for real estate agents is a requirement for renewing or maintaining a license in many states. It consists of classes or other activities that assist agents in staying updated with the most recent rules, legislation, fashions, and best practices in the real estate sector. As an agent, continuing education can also help you gain new abilities, broaden your knowledge, and improve your professionalism.

CHAPTER 2

COMPLETING THE AGENT PRE- LICENSING COURSE

A state-approved pre-licensing course must be the initial step in becoming a real estate agent. Most states require you to complete an agent course or get a degree with relevant subjects to pass the agent exam.

The pre-licensing education for agents is a set of courses that cover the basic knowledge and skills required to practice real estate. The topics may vary depending on the state or territory, but they usually include the following:

- Real estate principles and practices
- Real estate law and ethics
- Real estate finance and appraisal
- Real estate contracts and closing procedures
- Real estate marketing and sales techniques

Additional courses on particular subjects, such as fair housing, environmental concerns, or property management, may be required by some states or territories.

More precisely, the following steps are what you need to do:

CHOOSE A REPUTABLE AND ACCREDITED PROVIDER FOR THE COURSE

After knowing the expectations, enrolling in a reputable institution will help you develop the abilities you need and improve your chances of success. But, not all institutions that provide this training are equal. You must pick a recognized, accredited school up to industry and state standards.

Here's how you approach it.

1: Check the accreditation status of the school

Accreditation is a quality control process that guarantees the school satisfies specific requirements of excellence and abides by the moral and professional norms of the real estate industry. Therefore, you must ensure the state approves your chosen course and that the school satisfies the minimal licensing standards.

How can you check the accreditation status of the school or program that offers the pre-license course? Here is how:

- **Check your state's real estate commission website** - Most states have a list of approved schools and courses on their website. You can search by name, location, or type of course; this is the most reliable and official way to verify the accreditation status of a school or program.

- **Contact the school or program directly** - You can call, email, or visit the school or program and ask them about their accreditation status. They should be able to provide proof of approval from the state, such as a certificate, letter, or number. If they are unwilling or unable to do so, that should be cause for concern.

Choosing an accredited school or program for your pre-license course and save time and money. By following these steps, you can avoid wasting your time and money on a substandard or fraudulent curriculum.

2: Compare the curriculum and instructors of different schools

The pre-licensing course should cover every subject your state requires in the course, including real estate law, contracts, agency, financing, appraisal, ethics, and more.

Additionally, search for schools with educated and experienced teachers who can effectively instruct and prepare you for the test. Analyze the instructors' credentials and experience. You should seek out instructors with relevant degrees, qualifications, or licenses and actual work experience in the real estate sector. To learn more about their experience and teaching approach, look up their biographies, resumes, or LinkedIn profiles or contact them.

Learn about the subjects included in the curriculum, how thorough and current they are, and how long it takes to complete the program to compare the course content and length. For further information, visit the school's website or request a syllabus or course overview.

To obtain a sense of the classroom environment, the facilities, the resources, and the interactions between the teachers and other students, visit the school or sign up for a trial class.

You can schedule a school tour or sign up for a free or discounted trial class to see if it suits your needs and preferences.

3: Consider the format and schedule of the course

Depending on your preferences and availability, you can choose between an online course, an in- person course, or a course that combines both.

Online classes provide greater flexibility and convenience but require more motivation and self-control. Although in-person classes may be more expensive and time-consuming, they provide greater interaction and feedback. Additionally, you should confirm that the course's length and frequency match your learning style and objectives.

4: Compare the costs and benefits of different schools

Depending on the institution, the format, and the location, the fee of the pre- licensing course may change. Therefore, compare the tuition and other expenses like books, supplies, exam fees, etc.

Each institution's advantages, such as discounts, scholarships, payment plans, refunds, guarantees, support services, career coaching, etc., should also be key considerations. You should carefully consider the benefits and costs to choose which school will provide you with the best value for your money.

5: Read reviews and testimonials from alumni

Finding out what past students have to say about a school is one of the best ways to evaluate it. You might find the reviews and recommendations on the school's website, social media pages, blogs, forums, and review websites like Yelp and Google Reviews. Ask your friends, family, coworkers, or mentors for recommendations if they have taken the course or know someone who has.

Look for honest and fair reviews about the institution's advantages and disadvantages.

Making the right option when picking a reputable and approved institution for your pre- licensing course can greatly impact how successful you become as a real estate agent. You can pick a school that satisfies your needs and expectations and aids in achieving your career goals by using the above mentioned guidelines.

CHAPTER 3

HOW TO PASS YOUR FINAL EXAM AND GET YOUR LICENSE

The pre-agent licensing course exam is crucial in becoming a real estate agent. The exam will test your understanding of the rules, policies, and procedures governing real estate transactions. Therefore, you should review the course materials, do practice tests, and study the tough topic to prepare for the exam.

Additionally, familiarize yourself with the exam's structure, length, and grading scheme. The exam typically consists of multiple-choice questions and covers subjects like contract law, agency, financing, valuation, ethics, and disclosure.

You should also review your region's requirements and regulations because the exam may differ depending on your state. In most states, you need a minimum 70% or higher score to pass the exam. However, if you fail the exam, you may retake it after a specific time. Aim to ace the exam on your first try because doing so will save you time and money.

To prepare and pass your pre-agent licensing course exam, follow these steps:

REVIEW THE SYLLABUS AND THE LEARNING OBJECTIVES

If you are preparing for the final exam of your agent pre-licensing course, you might want to review the course's syllabus and learning objectives. You can then concentrate your study efforts and determine the key subjects covered in the exam by using these reliable sources of information.

Here are some tips on how to review them effectively:

- Start by looking at the syllabus and noting the course description, the learning outcomes, the assessment methods, and the grading criteria. These will provide you with an overview of the course's content, the lessons you should learn, the evaluation criteria, and the requirements you must meet.

- Next, review the learning goals for each module or course unit. These statements describe what you should be able to do or know by the end of each module or unit. The statements use verbs such as explain, analyze, apply, compare, etc. Try to understand what each objective means and how it relates to the course content and the exam questions.

- Finally, use the learning objectives to review the course materials, such as lectures, readings, assignments, quizzes, etc. For each objective, try to find relevant information in the materials and make notes or summaries of the key points. You can also use the objectives to test yourself or quiz a study partner on what you have learned.

Reviewing the syllabus and the learning objectives of your agent pre-licensing course can help you organize your study plan and improve your chances of passing the final exam. Remember to review them frequently and use them as a checklist to keep track of your development and spot any knowledge gaps.

MAKE A STUDY SCHEDULE AND FOLLOW IT

If you want to work in real estate, you must pass a pre-licensing course that teaches you the fundamentals of the field. Passing this course requires a solid study strategy because preparing for it might be difficult and time- consuming.

Here are some practical ways to make a study plan for your real estate agent pre-licensing course.

- **Set a realistic goal and timeline** - Before studying, you must know how much time you have until the exam and how much material you need to cover. You can use a calendar or a planner to mark the exam date and work backward from there. Divide the course content into manageable chunks and assign them specific days or weeks. Make sure you leave some buffer time for review and practice tests.

- **Choose a study method that suits your learning style**. There are different ways to study for the pre-licensing course, such as reading textbooks, watching videos, taking online courses, joining study groups, or hiring a tutor. Discover what works best for you and follow it religiously. For instance, using flashcards, pictures, or charts can be helpful if you learn best visually. Podcasts, lectures, or audiobooks might appeal more if you learn best through audio.

- **Create a conducive study environment** - You need a comfortable and distraction-free place to focus on your studies: your bedroom, home office, library, or coffee shop will all work. Ensure you have all the required supplies and equipment, including your laptop, notebooks, textbooks, highlighters, etc. Additionally, reduce any outside noise or interruptions, such as those from your phone, TV, family, etc.

- **Schedule regular study sessions and breaks** - You need a consistent and balanced study routine that fits your schedule and lifestyle. You can use a timer or an app to set specific study and rest periods. For example, you can follow the Pomodoro technique, which involves studying for 25 minutes and taking a 5-minute break. You can also adjust the length and frequency of your sessions and breaks according to your preference and energy level.

- **Review and test yourself frequently** - You need to reinforce what you have learned by reviewing and testing yourself regularly. You can review using various techniques, such as summarizing, rewriting, explaining, or instructing someone else on the subject. Other resources for testing oneself include quizzes, practice tests, flashcards, and online games. Aim to test yourself on the course material to determine your strengths and shortcomings.

- **Reward yourself and celebrate your achievements** - You need to have something that can keep you motivated and inspired throughout your study journey; this could be a system of incentives, a personal mantra, or a positive affirmation that serves as a reminder of your objectives and motivations for studying. By rewarding yourself with something you enjoy or sharing your success with others, you may also recognize your accomplishments, big or small.

REVIEW AND REVISE REGULARLY

When preparing for your real estate agent pre-licensing exam, you might feel anxious or overwhelmed by the material you need to master. Many aspiring agents face this difficulty, but with some clever tactics, you can resolve them.

Here are some doable strategies for studying and revising for the test while increasing your confidence.

- **Review the key concepts** - The real estate agent exam will test your knowledge of the fundamental concepts of real estate law, practice, and ethics. You need to review these concepts regularly and ensure you understand them well. You can use flashcards, summaries, or online resources to help you review the key concepts. Explain them in your own words and give examples of how they apply in real scenarios.

- **Revise the details** - Besides the key concepts, you must memorize some essential details for real estate practice, such as definitions, formulas, calculations, and regulations. To help you recall these specifics, you can employ songs, acronyms, and mnemonic devices. Making notes or diagrams can also help you remember by helping you to visualize it.

- **Take practice tests** - Taking practice exams that mimic the format and complexity of the real exam is one of the best ways to prepare for it. By taking practice exams, you can evaluate your strengths and shortcomings, find knowledge gaps, and develop test-taking techniques. You can find practice tests online, in books, or from your course provider. Take at least one practice test a week and review your answers carefully.

- **Seek feedback and support** - Studying for your exam can be stressful and lonely, but you don't have to do it alone. Ask your teachers, peers, mentors, or friends who are also studying for the test or have previously passed it for advice and assistance. You can also start a study group, ask them questions, or exchange advice. Communicate with other real estate agents and learn from their experiences by joining online forums or communities.

You can increase your knowledge, abilities, and self-assurance by using these realistic strategies for reviewing and revising for your exam. Remember that passing the exam is not only a matter of studying hard but also of studying smart.

Navigating the complex landscape of real estate exams requires not just diligence, but the right tools to guide one's study efforts. Several of my agents used Compucram, a dynamic and comprehensive exam preparation software, has emerged as an invaluable asset for many aspiring real estate agents. Tailored to match the specific content of state-based real estate exams, it offers a holistic approach to revision, blending interactive practice tests with timely feedback to identify areas of weakness. Its adaptive learning technology ensures that users are consistently challenged, reinforcing their knowledge and boosting their test-taking confidence. Many credit their success in passing the real estate exam to the rigorous preparation and real-time insights provided by Compucram, making it an indispensable ally in the journey towards becoming a licensed real estate professional.

HOW TO APPLY FOR YOUR AGENT LICENSE
AFTER PASSING THE EXAM

Congratulations on passing your exam! You have moved closer to obtaining a license and becoming a real estate agent. However, you must apply for your license and fulfill certain conditions before you may begin working as an agent. After passing the test, you must do the following to apply for your real estate agent license.

Submit your application and fee

After completing the post-licensing education, you can submit your application for your license to your state's real estate commission or department. You will have to present documentation of your identity, credentials, test results, and background checks. Additionally, there will be a cost that differs by state and might not be refundable.

For a complete list of qualifications and application deadlines, consult your state's specific webpage. The fees usually include an application fee, a license fee, and a fingerprint fee. You can pay these fees online or by mail.

Wait for processing and approval

Wait for your application to go through processing and approval after submission. Depending on your state and the number of applications they get, this could take a few days to a few weeks.

You can check the status of your application frequently to see if it has gone through—you can do this online or over the phone. Once your application is accepted, you will receive your license number and certificate by mail or email.

Maintain your license and continue your education

After getting your license, you need to maintain it by renewing it periodically and completing continuing education courses. The renewal period and the number of hours of continuing education vary by state, but they are usually required every one or two years.

You can find approved courses online or in person through your state's real estate commission or association. Grow your professional development through continuing education, which will inform you of the most recent real estate industry legislation, trends, and best practices.

CHAPTER 4

PICKING THE PERFECT REAL ESTATE BROKERAGE TO WORK WITH

Which brokerage to join is one of the most crucial, must-make choices as a new or aspiring real estate agent. A real estate brokerage is a business that hires agents and offers them access to listings, marketing assistance, training, and other services. Your choice of brokerage firm may significantly impact your career progress and job satisfaction.

There are many benefits of joining a brokerage that can help you succeed in your career. Below are some of the reasons why you should consider joining one:

- **Training and mentoring**: As a new agent, you need to learn the ropes of the industry, the regulations, the best practices, and the market trends. A brokerage can provide training and mentoring from experienced agents who can guide you and share their insights and tips. You can also benefit from the feedback and support of your peers and managers, who can help you improve your skills and performance.

- **Resources and tools**: A brokerage can offer access to various resources and tools to make your job easier and more efficient. For example, a brokerage can provide you with marketing materials, lead generation systems, CRM software, transaction management platforms, and more. You can also leverage the reputation and brand recognition of the brokerage to attract more clients and referrals.

- **Networking and opportunities**: A brokerage can help you expand your network and find more opportunities for your business. You can establish connections with other agents, lenders, appraisers, inspectors, attorneys, and other experts who can support your career. Events, workshops, seminars, webinars, and other activities can help you develop new skills, network with possible clients, and remain current on news and trends in your field.

- **Commission splits and fees**: A brokerage can offer you competitive commission splits and fees that can help you earn more income. Depending on the brokerage model, you might have to pay a monthly fee, a transaction fee, a desk fee, or a percentage of your commission to the brokerage. However, the value and benefits the brokerage provides will offset these fees. You should compare different brokerages and find the one that suits your needs and goals.

As you can see, joining a brokerage for a new agent can be a smart move that can help you grow in your career. However, not all brokerages are the same, so you should research and find the one that matches your personality, style, vision, and values.

Before deciding, you should consider each brokerage's culture, environment, support, training, resources, tools, network, opportunities, commission splits, and fees.

If you are a real estate agent looking for a brokerage to work with, you might be overwhelmed by the many options available. How can you pick the one that suits your personality, work style, and career objectives?

The following tips will help you choose the ideal real estate brokerage to work with.

RESEARCH DIFFERENT BROKERAGES IN YOUR AREA

Before joining a brokerage, you should consider various things, including commission splits, costs, culture, support, reputation, and opportunities.

Here is some advice on comparing brokerages in your area and choosing the one that best suits your needs and ambitions.

- **Start with online research** - You can use websites like Realtor.com, Zillow, or Trulia to browse listings in your area and see which brokerage firms are active and successful. You may also visit their websites and social media profiles to learn more about their branding, marketing, and principles. Check online reviews to discover what clients and agents have to say about their interactions with the broker. Also, attend brokerage open houses and events.

- **Narrow down your list** - Based on your online research, list brokerages that appeal to you and meet your criteria. You should consider size, location, specialty, education, technology, and culture. For example, do you prefer a large national franchise or a small local company? Do you want to work in a specific neighborhood or market segment? Do you need extensive training and mentoring or more autonomy and flexibility? Do you value a collaborative or competitive environment?

- **Schedule interviews** - Once you have a shortlist of brokerage, contact them and ask for an interview. You can discover more about the brokerage and determine whether it fits you well. Look for brokerages with a solid online presence, a sizable market share, and a decent reputation.

Many assume real estate agents must apply and compete for jobs at different brokerages, just like any other profession. However, this is not the case.

The agents interview and evaluate the brokerages and decide which suits their needs and goals best because agents are independent contractors, not employees, and must pay fees and commissions to their brokerages. Therefore, agents must choose which brokerage offers them the best value, support, training, and culture for their business.

RESEARCH THE REPUTATION AND CULTURE
OF THE BROKERAGE

One of the most important factors to consider is the reputation and culture of the brokerage. You want to work with a brokerage with a good market reputation, a strong brand identity, and a positive work culture.

But how do you research the reputation and culture of the brokerage before you join? Here are some practical ways to do that:

- **Ask other agents** - One of the best sources of information is the agents who work or have worked for the brokerage. You can contact them by phone, email, or social media and ask about their experience, satisfaction, and difficulties. Don't hesitate to ask detailed questions, but always be courteous and considerate.

- **Read online reviews** - Another way to understand the brokerage's reputation and culture is to read online reviews from clients, employees, and industry experts. You can use platforms like Google, Yelp, Glassdoor, or Indeed to find ratings, testimonials, and feedback. Pay attention to both positive and negative feedback, patterns, and trends.

- **Visit the office** - If possible, visit the brokerage's office in person and observe the atmosphere, layout, and interactions. You can also ask for a tour or a meeting with the broker or manager. You will observe how the brokerage functions, how the agents cooperate and communicate, and what resources and support they offer.

- **Attend events** - Another way to get a feel for the brokerage's culture is to attend events they host or participate in, such as open houses, seminars, webinars, or networking sessions. You may discover more about their principles, goals, and objectives, as well as their market standing and standing in the community. You can also interact with other agents and potential clients and get their impressions.

- **Do your homework** - Finally, research the brokerage's history, performance, and achievements. To learn more about their services, areas of expertise, honors, and recognition, visit their website, social media accounts, newsletters, or blogs. You can also check their license status, complaint history, and disciplinary actions with your state's real estate commission.

You may make an informed choice that will advance your career and help you reach your objectives by examining the brokerage's reputation and culture.

COMPARE THE COMMISSION SPLITS AND FEES

How much money you will make is a crucial consideration when picking a brokerage. You should carefully analyze the commission and fee structures various brokers offer to determine which best suits your spending needs and financial goals.

Commission splits are the percentage of the commission you receive from each transaction, while the rest goes to your broker. For example, if you sell a house for $300,000 and the commission is 6%, the total commission is $18,000. If your commission split is 70/30, you will receive 70% of $18,000, which is $12,600, while your broker will receive 30%, which is $5,400

Some brokers offer higher commission splits but charge more fees for marketing, training, technology, etc. Others offer lower commission splits but provide more support and resources. Consider the advantages and disadvantages of each choice to determine which is best for you.

Fees are the additional costs you must pay to your broker or the brokerage for various services and expenses. For example, some brokerages charge a monthly fee, a transaction fee, a desk fee, a marketing fee, or a technology fee. These fees vary widely across brokerages and significantly affect your net income.

To compare commission splits and fees across different brokerages, you need to consider several factors:

- **Your expected sales volume and price range** - If you expect to sell more or higher- priced properties, you might prefer a higher commission split over lower fees. However, if you expect to sell fewer or lower-priced properties, you might prefer lower fees over a higher commission split.

- **Your level of experience and support** - If you are a new agent who needs more training, mentoring, and guidance, you might be willing to accept a lower commission split in exchange for more support from your broker. However, if you are an experienced agent who can work independently and generate your leads, you might prefer a higher commission split and less support from your broker.

- **Your personal and business expenses** - If you have a lot of personal or business expenses, such as mortgage payments, car payments, insurance premiums, advertising costs, or office supplies, you might need a higher commission split to cover them. However, if you have fewer expenses or can reduce them by sharing them with other agents or using free or low-cost resources, you might be able to accept a lower commission split.

- **Your goals and preferences** - Ultimately, you must decide what matters most to you as an agent. Do you want to maximize your income or minimize your risk? Do you want to have more flexibility or more stability? Do you want to work with a large or small brokerage? Do you want to focus on a niche market or serve a broad clientele? These questions can help you determine what kind of commission split and fee structure suits your needs and aspirations.

You need to research and calculate to compare commission splits and fees effectively. Spreadsheets and commission calculators are examples of online tools to evaluate various scenarios and determine how they will affect your income. You can also inquire about the opinions and experiences of other brokerage agents. Additionally, you can conduct interviews with various brokers to learn more about their cultures, values, and expectations, as well as their commission splits and fees.

Comparing commission splits and fees is a challenging exercise, but it is one that new agents must complete to succeed in the real estate business. You can determine which professional path suits you by researching and carefully analyzing your possibilities.

EVALUATE THE TRAINING AND MENTORING OPPORTUNITIES

To succeed as a real estate agent, you must constantly learn new skills and be aware of recent trends and laws. Working with a brokerage that provides top- notch training and mentoring will help you expand your network and referrals while increasing your knowledge and confidence.

Look for a brokerage with a comprehensive training program, experienced mentors, and regular coaching sessions. You can enquire about their achievements and the endorsements of other agents who have benefited from their coaching and training.

But how can you evaluate the quality and effectiveness of different brokerages' training and mentoring programs? Here are some practical ways to do so:

- **Testimonials and feedback** - Ask for testimonials and feedback from current or former agents participating in the training and mentoring programs. Learn about their experiences with the programs, the benefits, and how they used what they learned to grow their real estate career.

- **Review the curriculum and content of the training and mentoring programs** - Look for relevant, up-to-date, and comprehensive topics. You might wish to research market trends, lead generation, contract negotiations, marketing, technology, ethical concerns, and legal matters. Additionally, confirm if the programs suit your unique needs and objectives as a new agent.

- **Assess the trainers' and mentors' qualifications and experience** - Look for credentials demonstrating their expertise and credibility in the real estate industry. For example, you may want to look for certifications, awards, testimonials, referrals, or reviews. Additionally, find out whether they have a history of success as agents and if they can offer you continuing help and support.

- **Compare the costs and benefits of the training and mentoring programs** - Find out how much you have to pay for the programs and what you get in return. For example, you may want to consider the programs' duration, frequency, format, and delivery method. Also, check for additional resources or perks that come with the programs, such as access to tools, systems, networks, or leads.

- **Try out the training and mentoring programs before you commit** - Many brokerages offer free or discounted trial sessions or introductory courses that allow you to experience their training and mentoring programs first-hand; this might help you get a sense of the programs' quality and style to determine whether they meet your standards and tastes.

ASSESS THE TECHNOLOGY AND TOOLS AVAILABLE

Today's real estate industry depends heavily on technology since it may help you organize your work, interact with clients, market your listings, and create leads.

You want to deal with a brokerage that gives you access to the newest tools and technologies to support your success. A user-friendly website, a reliable CRM system, a strong lead generation system, a mobile app, and social media integration are some of the systems to look for.

As a new agent, you might be overwhelmed by the variety of technology and tools available from different brokerages. How can you assess the best suits your needs and goals?

Here are some tips to help you evaluate the technology and tools offered by different brokerages:

- **Compare the features and benefits of each technology and tool** - What are the main functions and advantages? How do they help you generate leads, manage transactions, communicate with clients, market yourself, and grow your business? How easy are they to use and learn? How reliable and secure are they?

- **Ask for a demo or a trial period** - Before you commit to a brokerage, you should be able to test their technology and tools. Ask for a demo or a trial period to access and use their platforms and software; this will enable you to see how they operate and whether they complement your workflow and personal preferences.

- **Seek feedback from other agents** - Another way to assess the technology and tools is by asking other agents who have utilized the technology for their opinions. You can get advice and referrals from coworkers, friends, mentors, and online communities. Additionally, you can read evaluation reports and reviews from other brokers on websites, blogs, social media, or discussion forums.

- **Consider the costs and value of each technology and tool** - Finally, you should consider each technology and tool offered by different brokerages. How much do they charge for their services and products? Are there any hidden fees or contracts? What is each technology and tool's return on investment (ROI)? How do they help you save time, money, or resources?

CONSIDER THE LOCATION AND SIZE OF THE BROKERAGE

Choosing the right brokerage can greatly impact your success and satisfaction as a real estate agent.

But how do you find the perfect brokerage for you? There are many factors to consider, such as commission splits, fees, culture, reputation, and opportunities. However, two of the most crucial factors are location and size.

Let's see why they matter and how to evaluate them.

Location

Location is important for two reasons: convenience and market. You want to join a conveniently located brokerage so you can easily access the office, attend meetings, network with other agents, and use the facilities. A long commute can waste time and money and reduce productivity and motivation.

You also want to join a brokerage with a strong presence in your target market. If you want to specialize in a particular real estate area or niche, you need to work with a brokerage with a good reputation and track record in that market; this will help you attract more clients, get more referrals, and close more deals.

To evaluate the location of a brokerage, you should consider the following questions:

- How far is the office from your home?
- How easy is it to get there by car or public transportation?
- How much parking is available?
- How close is the office to your target market?
- How well-known and respected is the brokerage in your target market?
- How many listings and sales does the brokerage have in your target market?

Size

Size is an important factor when it comes to choosing a brokerage. The size of a brokerage can affect the level of support, training, resources, and competition you will experience as an agent.

Generally, larger brokerages offer more support, training, and resources than smaller ones. They might have greater resources like employees, marketing, technology, and equipment to support the business. They might also have a larger market share and brand awareness, which could provide you an advantage over other agents.

However, larger brokerages may also have more fees, rules, and bureaucracy than smaller ones. They may have less flexibility and autonomy for their agents. They may also have more competition and pressure among their agents, affecting your income and morale.

Smaller brokerages offer more flexibility, autonomy, and personal attention than larger ones. They may have fewer fees, rules, and bureaucracy to deal with. Additionally, they might have more cooperation and camaraderie among their agents, which can foster a productive and encouraging work atmosphere.

However, smaller brokerages may offer less support, training, and resources than larger ones. They may have less staff, technology, marketing, and tools to help you grow your business. They might also have a smaller market share and less name recognition, making it more difficult for you to compete with other agents for clients.

To evaluate the size of a brokerage, you should consider the following questions:

- How many agents work for the brokerage?
- How much support, training, and resources does the brokerage provide?
- How much fees, rules, and bureaucracy does the brokerage impose?
- How much flexibility and autonomy does the brokerage allow?
- How much competition and pressure does the brokerage create?

- How much camaraderie and collaboration does the brokerage foster?

As discussed earlier, the best way to find the answers to these questions is to do online research, ask other agents who have worked there, or even make inquiries with the brokerage and get answers to all these questions.

CHAPTER 5

HOW TO DEVELOP YOUR SKILLS AND KNOWLEDGE AS A REAL ESTATE AGENT

Your success as a real estate agent depends on your ability to offer your clients outstanding service, close the best deals, and keep up with market developments. Since real estate is highly competitive and dynamic, agents must have various skills and knowledge.

To be a successful real estate agent, you need more than a license and a love of selling homes. Additionally, you require critical skills and knowledge that will let you stand out from the crowd and offer your clients value. Market knowledge, communication, marketing, technological, and negotiation skills are some of the skills.

These are some of the most crucial skills and information every successful real estate agent should possess. You may raise your chances of reaching your objectives and meeting your client's needs by enhancing and developing these skills and knowledge.

But how do you maintain your skill and knowledge advancement in this cutthroat and fast-paced industry?

Here are some pointers to help you advance professionally and meet your job objectives.

HOW TO IMPROVE YOUR MARKET KNOWLEDGE

Market awareness is critical for every real estate agent wishing to succeed in this ever- changing business. Understanding current trends, demands, opportunities, and obstacles in the local and international real estate marketplaces is called having market knowledge.

Additionally, it entails being aware of the traits, preferences, and requirements of various consumer and seller types and the variables that affect their choices.

To help improve your market knowledge, you can:

- **Conduct regular market research and analysis** - This involves collecting and interpreting data from various sources, such as online platforms, industry reports, media outlets, government agencies, trade associations, and professional networks. The information must encompass market size, expansion, segmentation, supply and demand, pricing, rivalry, laws, and innovations.

- **Stay updated on the latest news and developments in the real estate industry** - This involves reading, watching, or listening to relevant publications, podcasts, webinars, blogs, newsletters, and social media posts from reputable and authoritative sources. The information should cover market trends, best practices, success stories, challenges, opportunities, and forecasts.

- **Network with other real estate professionals and experts** - This involves attending or participating in events, seminars, workshops, conferences, and forums related to the real estate industry. The interactions should aim to exchange insights, opinions, experiences, and referrals with peers, mentors, leaders, and influencers.

- **Seek feedback from clients and prospects** - This involves asking for their opinions, preferences, expectations, and satisfaction levels regarding the real estate services and products they have received or are interested in. Use feedback to determine the market's advantages, disadvantages, opportunities, and threats.

- **Visit properties and neighborhoods** - Nothing beats the experience of visiting properties and neighborhoods in person. You can look at different properties' features, amenities, conditions, and prices. You can also observe the demographics, culture, lifestyle, and demand of different neighborhoods; this can help you develop a sense of each property and area's market value and potential.

HOW TO IMPROVE YOUR COMMUNICATION SKILLS AS A REAL ESTATE AGENT

Any real estate agent who wants to succeed in the competitive market must have excellent communication skills. Building trust, rapport, and credibility with your clients, prospects, and coworkers may be done with the use of effective communication.

Here are some suggestions for enhancing your communication ability as a real estate agent.

- **Listen actively and empathetically** - One of the most important aspects of communication is listening. You must consider your customers' requirements, tastes, objectives, and worries.

Additionally, you must pay attention to their comments, objections, and inquiries. Active listening means paying attention, asking relevant questions, and paraphrasing what you heard to confirm understanding. Empathetic listening means showing genuine interest, respect, and compassion for your clients' emotions and perspectives.

- **Adapt your communication style to your audience** - Different people have different communication styles, preferences, and expectations. You must tailor your communication style to suit your listener and the situation.

  For example, some clients may prefer a formal and professional tone, while others may appreciate a friendly and casual one. Some prefer detailed information and explanations, while others want clear and precise summaries. Some clients may respond well to humor and stories, while others may find them inappropriate or distracting.

- **Use clear and concise language** - Avoid jargon, slang, or technical terms your clients may not understand. Use straightforward language that conveys your message clearly and accurately. Avoid using filler words, such as "um," "like," or "you know." Use short and simple sentences that are easy to follow and comprehend. Use transitions, such as "first," "next," or "finally," to organize your thoughts and guide your listeners.

- **Use nonverbal communication effectively** - Nonverbal communication includes your body language, facial expressions, eye contact, gestures, posture, and tone of voice. Nonverbal communication can enhance or undermine your verbal communication. Use nonverbal communication that matches your verbal message and shows confidence, professionalism, and enthusiasm. For example, you can use a smile, a nod, or a handshake to show friendliness and rapport. Use eye contact to show interest and attention, and use a firm and clear voice to show authority and competence.

- **Seek feedback and improve continuously** - Communication is a two-way process that requires constant evaluation and improvement. Ask your clients, prospects, coworkers, and mentors for comments on your communication style. You can ask them for specific recommendations on what you did right and wrong. You can also study the communication techniques of other successful real estate agents by watching them.

HOW TO BUILD AND IMPROVE YOUR MARKETING SKILLS

Real estate agents know the importance of marketing in attracting and keeping clients, generating leads, and closing deals. But how can you become more competitive by honing your marketing abilities?

One of the most crucial abilities for a real estate agent is marketing. It can assist you in gaining new clients, showcasing your knowledge, and establishing credibility.

Some tips to help you achieve that include:

- **Learn from the best** - Find the top real estate agents in your area or niche and study their marketing strategies. What channels do they use? What kind of content do they share? How do they communicate their value proposition? Another alternative would be following industry leaders, influencers, and experts on social media, blogs, podcasts, and newsletters and learning from what they say.

- **Invest in your online presence** - A professional and user-friendly website is essential for any real estate agent. You can showcase your listings, testimonials, awards, and credentials. It's also where you can generate leads, capture email addresses, and nurture relationships with potential clients. Ensure that your website is speedy, mobile- friendly, and search engine-optimized. You can track the effectiveness of your website and find areas for improvement using tools like Google Analytics.

- **Leverage social media** - Social media is a powerful tool for real estate agents to reach and engage with their target audience. You may post useful content, including market updates, tips, trends, tales, videos, live streams, and more, on websites and apps like Facebook, Instagram, Twitter, LinkedIn, YouTube, and TikTok. You can engage with your clients on social media, respond to their queries, request their opinions, and present your personality and brand.

- **Create a blog or a newsletter** - A blog or a newsletter is a great way to establish yourself as an authority and a thought leader in your field. You can use it to share your knowledge, thoughts, perceptions, and suggestions on real estate-related subjects. It can also inform your audience, solve their problems, and offer answers. You can use a blog or newsletter to increase reader trust, loyalty, and rapport while bringing visitors to your website and generating leads.

- **Experiment with different formats and channels** - Marketing is not a one-size-fits- all approach. Different formats and channels may work better for audiences, goals, and messages. For example, you may want to use video to showcase a property tour or a testimonial; you may want to use email to send personalized offers or follow-ups; you may want to use podcasts to interview guests or share stories; you may want to use webinars to host workshops or Q&A sessions. Test many choices to determine which ones work best for you and your audience.

These suggestions can help develop and enhance your real estate agent marketing abilities and expand your firm.

HOW TO IMPROVE YOUR NEGOTIATION SKILLS

Any real estate agent who wants to prosper in this fast-paced market must have negotiation skills. Building connection, trust, and loyalty with the purchasers are all important aspects of negotiation and securing the best possible price for your customers. Your ability to negotiate can set you apart from other agents and help you and your agency build a solid reputation.

Here are some suggestions to aid you in sharpening your negotiating abilities:

Know your buyers

One of the first steps to effective negotiation is to know who you are dealing with. Different buyers have different needs, preferences, motivations, and personalities. You must do your homework and research your buyers before meeting them.

Find out as much as possible about their background, financial situation, goals, expectations, and pain points. You can learn all this by asking them questions before beginning the negotiation (BATNA) (Fisher, Ury, & Patton, 2011)i.

Some examples of questions you can ask your clients to know them better and tailor your service to their expectations include the following:

- Why are you looking for a property now?
- How long have you been looking for a property?
- What is your budget, and how do you plan to finance your purchase?

These questions will help you tailor your approach and communication style to suit each buyer.

For example, if you are selling to a first-time buyer, you might want to emphasize the benefits of homeownership, such as stability, security, and equity. You may also offer more guidance and support throughout the process because the person might be unfamiliar with the legal and technical aspects of buying a home.

On the other hand, if you are selling to an investor, you might want to focus on the property's return on investment, cash flow, and appreciation potential. In addition, you may also want to use more data and facts to back up your claims because an investor might be more analytical and rational.

Listen actively

Another key skill for successful negotiation is active listening. Active listening means paying attention to what the buyer says and their body language, tone of voice, and emotions.

Active listening shows that you care about the buyer's needs and concerns and are willing to understand their perspective. You may use the information you learn about the buyer's priorities, interests, and hot buttons to strengthen your position by actively listening to them.

For example, suppose you notice that the buyer is interested in the property's location. In that case, you can highlight the advantages of living in that area, such as convenience, amenities, and lifestyle. You can also mention some testimonials or referrals from other satisfied buyers who live in the same neighborhood.

On the other hand, if you notice that the buyer is very concerned about the property's price, you can explain the property's value proposition, such as its features, quality, and potential. Additionally, you can demonstrate how it provides a superior deal by contrasting it with other comparable properties on the market.

Ask open-ended questions

A third way to improve your negotiation skills is to ask open-ended questions. Open-ended questions are questions that require more than a yes or no answer. They encourage the buyer to share more information, opinions, and feelings about the property and the deal. You can learn more about the buyer's needs, wants, objections, and hesitations by asking open- ended inquiries.

Additionally, by posing open-ended queries, you demonstrate your interest in getting to know the client better and your respect for their opinions.

For example, instead of asking, "Do you like this property?" which will prompt a simple yes or no, you can ask, "What do you like most about this property?" or "How do you see yourself living in this property?". These questions will elicit more detailed and personal responses from the buyer, which you can use to build rapport and trust.

Similarly, instead of asking, "Are you ready to make an offer?" which can put pressure on the buyer and make them defensive, you can ask, "What are your thoughts on making an offer?" or "What would it take for you to make an offer?". These questions invite the buyer to share their concerns and expectations, which you can address and overcome.

Use positive language

A fourth tip to enhance your negotiation skills is to use positive language. Positive language is the language that expresses optimism, confidence, and enthusiasm. Positive language can influence the buyer's mood, attitude, and perception of the property and the deal. Positive language can also help create a win-win situation where both parties feel satisfied and valued.

For example, instead of saying, "This is the final price," which sounds rigid and aggressive, you can say, "This is a great opportunity," which sounds inviting and appealing. Instead of saying, "You have to decide by tomorrow," which sounds urgent and stressful, you can say, "You don't want to miss this chance," which sounds encouraging and motivating.

Be flexible

A fifth way to improve your negotiation skills is to be flexible. Flexibility means adapting to the buyer's changing circumstances and preferences. Flexibility also means compromise and finding common ground with the buyer. Flexibility shows you are open-minded, cooperative, and solution- oriented. Flexibility can help you avoid deadlock situations and reach a mutually beneficial agreement.

For example, if the buyer is not willing to budge on the price, you can offer some concessions on other terms, such as closing date, inspection, repairs, or contingencies. You can suggest creative solutions like seller financing, lease options, or rent-to-own. You can also ask the buyer what they will give up or trade in exchange for a lower price.

Negotiation skills are essential for any real estate agent who wants to succeed in the business. Using these useful recommendations, you may sharpen your bargaining abilities and get greater results for yourself and your clients. Remember to know your buyers, listen actively, ask open-ended questions, use positive language, and be flexible. These skills will help you stand out and build lasting relationships with your buyers.

HOW TO LEVERAGE THE POWER OF TECHNOLOGY TO BECOME A BETTER REAL ESTATE AGENT

The ever-evolving technology has completely affected how we live, work and communicate. Additionally, it has altered how we buy and sell houses. That's why you must stay updated with the newest tools and trends in real estate to expand your clientele and improve your business.

In this section, we'll look at ways you may use technology to improve your productivity, effectiveness, and success as a real estate agent.

- **Use a CRM system to manage your contacts, leads, and transactions** - A CRM system can help organize your data, track your communication, automate your follow-ups, and generate reports. A CRM system can also help you personalize your marketing activities and give your customers better service.

According to a study by the National Association of Realtors (NAR), 26% of agents who use a CRM system earn more than $100,000 per year, compared to 10% of agents who do not use one (NAR, 2019)ii.

Other best software systems that can help you become a better real estate agent include:

- **Zillow Premier Agent**: This powerful platform connects you with millions of buyers and sellers who use Zillow to search for properties. You can create a profile, showcase your listings, receive leads, and track your performance. Zillow Premier Agent also offers advertising options, coaching programs, and market insights to help you grow your business.

- **HubSpot CRM**: This is a free and easy- to-use CRM system that helps you manage your contacts, deals, tasks, and activities. Additionally, you can link HubSpot CRM with other HubSpot technologies, like analytics, landing pages, email marketing, and more. HubSpot CRM enables you to automate activities, streamline workflow, and nurture leads.

- **Dotloop**: This comprehensive transaction management system helps you create, share, and sign documents online. You can also collaborate with your clients, team members, and other parties involved in the deal. Dotloop helps you save time, reduce errors, and stay compliant. To cite Dotloop in APA referencing style, you can use the following format:

- **Create a professional website and social media presence** - A website and social media presence can help showcase your listings, demonstrate your expertise, and build trust with your prospects and clients. A website and social media presence can also help you generate more leads, referrals, and reviews. According to NAR, 51% of buyers found their homes online, and 77% of sellers found their agents online (NAR, 2020) iii. Therefore, having a strong online presence is essential for attracting and retaining clients.

- **Use video marketing to engage your audience and showcase your properties** - Video marketing can help you capture your audience's attention, convey your personality, and highlight the features and benefits of your properties. Video marketing can also help you increase your reach, as videos are more likely to be shared on social media than other types of content. According to NAR, 85% of buyers and sellers would prefer to work with an agent who uses video marketing (NAR, 2018)iv.

  This shows you must create a video tour of your listings to give viewers a better sense of a property's space, layout, and features. You can also highlight the benefits and unique selling points of each listing, such as the location, amenities, or design.

  Include client testimonials and reviews in your video to create credibility and authority in your field and demonstrate how you can help your clients reach their goals. You can ask your past or current clients to record a short video testimonial about their experience working with you and share it on your website, social media, or email newsletter.

To inform your audience on the real estate market, the buying or selling process, or any other subjects pertinent to your niche, provide them with useful tips and guidance. For instance, you may offer advice on getting the best mortgage rate, negotiating a contract, or preparing a house for sale. This strategy might assist you in establishing yourself as an authority figure and reliable source for your audience.

- **Use virtual and augmented reality to enhance your property tours** - Virtual and augmented reality can help you provide immersive and interactive experiences for your clients. Virtual and augmented reality can also help you save time and money because you can show multiple properties in one session without traveling. According to NAR, 77% of buyers would use virtual or augmented reality to view a home remotely, and 63% of sellers would use it to stage their home (NAR, 2017)v.

These are just a few examples of how you can use technology to your advantage to improve yourself as a real estate agent and differentiate yourself from the competition. You may get a competitive edge in the market and give your clients more value by employing technology intelligently and creatively.

CHAPTER 6

COMMON PROBLEMS NEW REAL ESTATE AGENTS FACE AND HOW TO OVERCOME THEM

Real estate agent careers can be fulfilling and lucrative but also present unique difficulties and hardships. Whether you are just starting or have been in the business for a while, you will most likely encounter some common problems that new real estate agents face.

Here are some of the most common issues that new agents face and some tips on how to deal with them effectively:

LACK OF LEADS

One of the biggest challenges for new agents is finding and generating leads. You will struggle to close deals and earn commissions if you don't have a steady stream of potential clients.

You must invest in your physical and online marketing to address this issue. You can market yourself and draw leads via social media, websites, blogs, newsletters, flyers, signs, referrals, networking events, open homes, and more.

According to Qobrix (2023)vi, having a strong online strategy is critical in getting prospects to see your real estate portfolio because 97% of home buyers searched the Internet for homes in 2021 (NARS, 2021). Additionally, you must consistently follow up with your leads and give them useful details and support.

LOW CONVERSION RATE

Another common problem for new agents is converting leads into clients. You may have a lot of contacts, but if they are not interested in buying or selling a property with you, they will not help you grow your business.

To solve this issue, qualify your leads and concentrate on those most likely to lead to closed deals. You can use online tools like CRM systems to track and manage your leads and their preferences. You can establish rapport and trust by paying attention to your leads' needs, giving them pertinent information, and demonstrating your expertise.

HIGH COMPETITION

The real estate industry is highly competitive and saturated with agents vying for the same clients and properties. You may struggle to stand out from the crowd and differentiate yourself from your competitors.

To solve this issue, you must create a distinctive value proposition and a personal brand highlighting your abilities, experience, personality, and specialization. Additionally, you should play to your strengths and concentrate on the areas where you are particularly strong, such as a specific market sector, property type, or service line. Also, you must stay updated with market trends and technological advancements and apply them to improve your service delivery and customer happiness.

LOW INCOME

One of the most frustrating problems for new agents is earning a low or no income. Real estate is a commission-based business where you only get paid when you close a deal; this can be unpredictable and inconsistent, especially when you are new to the industry and have not built a solid client base yet.

Establish reasonable expectations to solve this issue for yourself and your business. You should also create a budget and track your expenses and income carefully. You should also diversify your income sources by offering additional services or products, such as staging, photography, consulting, etc.

BURNOUT

One of the most serious problems for new agents is experiencing burnout. Much time, effort, dedication, and grit are needed to succeed in the stressful and demanding real estate field. You may feel overwhelmed by the workload, pressure, deadlines, rejections, conflicts, and emotions involved in the business.

Address your physical, mental, emotional, and spiritual needs to solve this issue. Also balance your work and personal life by setting boundaries, prioritizing tasks, delegating responsibilities, outsourcing tasks, taking breaks, relaxing, exercising, sleeping well, eating healthy, meditating, etc.

These are some of the typical issues new real estate brokers run with, along with solutions. You may improve your chances of success and fulfillment as a real estate agent by being aware of these difficulties and taking proactive measures to solve them.

CONCLUSION

Choosing a real estate agent career can be enjoyable because it has numerous advantages, like flexibility, freedom, and endless earning potential. But it also calls for perseverance, hard work, and ongoing education.

As you reach the end of this eBook, know that your journey in real estate is just beginning. If you're seeking personalized guidance, mentorship, or insights tailored to your unique situation, I invite you to reach out. My commitment to empowering aspiring real estate professionals extends beyond these pages. Feel free to connect with me for one-on-one consulting at info@beyourownbroker.org. Let's navigate the dynamic world of real estate together, ensuring your path is not just successful, but also enriching. Wishing you unparalleled success in all your real estate endeavors!

REFERENCES

i   Fisher, R., Ury, W., & Patton, B. (2011). Getting to yes: Negotiating agreement without giving in (3rd ed.). Penguin Books.

ii   NAR. (2019). Real estate technology: What's new for 2019? Retrieved from https://www.nar.realtor/reports/real-estate-technology- whats-new-for-2019

iii NAR. (2020). Real estate in a virtual world: How COVID-19 transformed the industry. Retrieved from https://www.nar.realtor/reports/real-estate-in-a-virtual-world

iv NAR. (2018). The digital house hunt: Consumer and market trends in real estate. Retrieved from https://www.nar.realtor/sites/default/files/documents/2018- real-estate-in-a-digital-age-03-14-2018.pdf

v   NAR. (2017). Real estate in a digital age. Retrieved from https://www.nar.realtor/sites/default/files/reports/2017/2017-real-estate-in-a-digital-age- 03-10-2017.pdf

vi Qobrix. (2023). 7 top challenges facing realtors in 2023. Retrieved from https://qobrix.com/2023/01/09/the-top-7-challenges-facing-realtors-in-2023/

MY NOTES

MY NOTES

MY NOTES

MY NOTES

MY NOTES

MY NOTES

MY NOTES

MY NOTES

MY NOTES

www.ingramcontent.com/pod-product-compliance
Lightning Source LLC
Chambersburg PA
CBHW062248290526
45794CB00006B/2452